Every Phoneme Covered

A complete Synthetic Phonics resource using simple sentences, stories and poems

Steve Way and Simon Hickton

Hopscotch

A division of MA Education Ltd.

Hopscotch

A division of MA Education Ltd

Published by Hopscotch,
a division of MA Education,
St Jude's Church, Dulwich Road,
London, SE24 0PB
www.hopscotchbooks.com
020 7738 5454

© 2011 MA Education Ltd

Written by Steve Way and Simon Hickton
Illustrated by Brian Way
Designed by Claire White, Fonthill Creative

ISBN 978 1 90751 541 5

Contents

Introduction...6

Teachers' Notes...8
Terminology..9
The Text Resources...10
Using the Resource...12
Sample Texts...19–22

Word List...23
Consonants..23–35
Vowels and Dipthongs..35–47

Appendix
Index for Word List...48
Summary of Phonemes and their Graphemes.................50
Teaching Order..54

Introduction

This book dovetails with the "Letters and Sounds" programme as it supports high quality phonics work within a broad and rich language curriculum, as encouraged by the "Letters and Sounds" philosophy.

"It is important to demonstrate reading and writing in context every day to make sure that children apply their phonic knowledge when reading and writing in their role-play and other chosen activities." *

Every Phoneme Covered provides written pieces of increasing complexity focussing on each phoneme. These allow children to develop specific reading and writing skills far more easily than by using normal texts.

By working with the text resources in various ways, children can learn the skill of relating graphemes to phonemes when reading and phonemes to graphemes when speaking, writing and spelling.

The "Letters and Sounds" programme is based on the "simple view of reading" outlined in the "Rose Report"** which suggests that the major factors supporting development of reading skills are learning language comprehension processes and word recognition processes. It is anticipated that developing a child's word recognition skill through developing the knowledge of phonics will contribute to that aspect of their developing reading skill. By utilising the texts in this resource, children can simultaneously develop their language comprehension, reading, writing and vocabulary skills.

Use of a "multi-sensory" approach is encouraged by the advocates of the "Letters and Sounds" publication. The text pieces are useful teaching tools because they can be utilised in such a variety of contexts. Children can interact with the pieces in many ways, for example by reading them, having them read to them, searching out phonemes/

graphemes within them, creating dramas, pictures related to the stories or writing their own stories, to name just a few.

The various pieces within **Every Phoneme Covered** can support all six phases of the Letters and Sounds programme, even phase one which requires children to have *"a broad and rich language experience"* [*].

The resource can also be useful in KS2 (age 7 – 11) to help development of spelling ability, which usually lags behind development of reading skills.

The "Letters and Sounds" programme highlights which phonemes/graphemes need to be worked on at each stage; **Every Phoneme Covered** provides texts of varying complexity, thus supporting the different levels of ability.

*Letters and Sounds: Notes of Guidance for Practitioners and Teachers. Primary National Strategy 00282–2007BKT–EN

**Independent Review of teaching of early reading, Final Report, Jim Rose 2006

Teachers' Notes

For years teachers have skillfully used a variety of methods, techniques and resources to ensure that the vast majority of children become literate.

The texts provided on the CD of **Every Phoneme Covered** will support the children as they learn to read and write.

More and more research is showing that children do need a basic framework to support their reading and writing development and that using synthetic phonics as a tool can support this. This certainly matches our own class teaching experience.

Synthetic phonics involve isolating and blending phonemes and their grapheme choices. Analytic phonics involve analysing common phonemes in a set of words, which is still a useful tool even though synthetic phonics is the main driving force for teaching phonics and is the current emphasis of educational practice.

We have taken 43 sounds (phonemes) of the English language and their spelling (grapheme) choices and created texts to provide materials to aid the learning and teaching of reading and writing. Our texts are based on a synthetic phonics approach and therefore work alongside any good phonics framework or resource that is used in school.

Our resource incorporates an understanding of how children learn and remember and the pieces are ideal for incorporating into accelerated learning techniques. They can be utilised in many ways and we have used them, and seen them used, throughout the primary age range.

Steve Way and Simon Hickton

Terminology

Good frameworks and resources recommend the use of the correct terminology from the start. Children do not have a problem with this. They can all remember and pronounce, for example, a lot more Star Wars, dinosaur or Bionicle names than we ever could!

- — - — - — - — - — - — - — - — - — - — - — - — - — - — - — - —

Phoneme: A speech sound

An **allophone** is a variant of a particular phoneme e.g. the exploded t sound of top and the unexploded one in the middle of later are allophones of the phoneme /t/. These may be pronounced differently in different regions, due to the rich diversity of regional accents. Note. A syllable is a unit of pronunciation representing the vowel phonemes in words, e.g. cat has one syllable (but three phonemes), water has two syllables (but four phonemes) and inferno has three syllables (but six phonemes).

Grapheme: Letter or letters that represent a phoneme, these are spelling choices.

Graphemes can be subdivided into:

Graph: A single letter showing one phoneme.

Digraph: Two letters showing one phoneme.

Trigraph: Three letters showing one phoneme.

Split Digraph: Two letters separated by another letter showing one phoneme.

Examples

The c, a and t in cat are all graphs.

The ai in rain and ch in school are digraphs.

The dge in bridge and igh in light are trigraphs.

The a–e in name is a split digraph.

The sounds used in the English language can be divided up into, arguably,* 43 or 44 phonemes, 24 consonant phonemes and 19 or 20 vowel phonemes, along with their grapheme choices. "Grapheme choices" are the graphemes that can represent a single phoneme.

E.g.: c, k, ck, ch & q are the grapheme choices for the phoneme /c/ as it sounds in the words cat, kitten, duck, school and queen.

f, ff & ph are the grapheme choices for the phoneme /f/ as it sounds in the words fish, coffee and dolphin.

Reading is the conversion of **graphemes** into **phonemes**.

Spelling is the conversion of **phonemes** into **graphemes** and thus relies heavily upon visual memory. "Does it look right?"

Diphthong is a vowel phoneme in which the articulation begins as for one vowel phoneme and moves towards another e.g. oi in coin (starts as o, changes to i.)

— —

* The "44th" phoneme ʊə /oor/ is used so infrequently that it's not included in this resource. There aren't enough words using it to write anything with! The Literacy Framework does not acknowledge this phoneme either.

The Text Resources on the CD

This resource is in the form of three pieces of text for 43 phonemes and their grapheme choices. All three forms of text are on the CD. By using the CD the pieces can be displayed directly onto whiteboards or printed onto paper for group or individual use.

1. Fantastic Phoneme

– A very simple memory cue or cues in the form of a short comical sentence to help children remember words which contain the graphemes of a particular phoneme.

In general we see this resource as being useful for 5 to 8 year old children, but it can be used for younger or older children as well. As with all the resources, some of the phonemes covered will be used more than others, but there are resources for each phoneme so a wide spectrum of ability can be served by using these sentences. It is important to show children the whole picture, as many need to see this before they can start to make sense of our complicated language. Using these sentences allows the children to encounter the phonemes they are learning in a meaningful context.

2. Grab the Graphemes

– A short simple text with lots of words which contain a particular phoneme's grapheme choices.

In general we would see this resource as being useful for teacher-guided activities for 5 to 7 year old children and more independent work for 8 to 11 year olds. The idea of using texts is that the children will gain a broader experience of using words incorporating particular phonemes in a wider context than when using the single sentences of the 'Fantastic Phonemes'. The pieces have deliberately been kept quite short so that children beginning to gain confidence in reading and writing are not overfaced by them and will be able to imagine being able to write pieces of a similar length.

3. Phoneme Fable

– A more advanced text for stretching more confident readers with lots of words which contain a particular phoneme.

In general we would see this resource as being appropriate for use with children of a reasonable reading age, about 8 to 11 years. Work using these pieces will help the children develop their knowledge of and confidence in using phonetics as a tool to building advanced linguistic skills, synthesised in context with other language skills that the children may be developing simultaneously. It will be particularly useful for supporting those children who may have learned to read confidently, but do not spell confidently. Even for children with advanced language skills, they will help hone and develop these skills as the 'Phoneme Fables' use a very wide range of different genres.

We would suggest that there is a lack of resources to help 9 to 11 year old children continue building the phonetics skills developed in previous years. Certainly there are no formats that are appropriate to the age and associated skills development of older children and other children still struggling to read at an appropriate level for their age. We suggest that the 'Phoneme Fables' represent a means of plugging that previously existing resources gap. It could also support older juniors for whom English is a second language.

From the beginning of this project we felt all texts emphasising the use of particular phonemes would give children an opportunity to develop their reading and spelling skills. At the same time they would be able to practise key reading skills such as knowledge of context and grammar and word recognition. All good texts facilitate learning these latter skills, but we agreed with a National Literacy Strategy publication, ('Phonics' 2001) which stated that: *"In most texts phonic patterning occurs too randomly to be discerned"*. We hope that our resource remedies this deficiency.

We have cited the I.P.A. (International Phonetic Alphabet) symbol for each phoneme, as these are often used for reference, e.g. in the Oxford English Dictionary. This may come in useful when you are list building and want to rapidly check that a word does use the phoneme you are looking for. We've also noted the symbols used by the Primary Framework for Literacy 2006 and the "Letters and Sounds" publication 2007 (referred to as "L. & S.").

Using the Resource

We see this as an extremely versatile resource, so the suggestions we've made below are only some of the ways in which you may decide to use the resource.

The examples below show how the resource can be used across the age range. Where specific examples are given we've used lessons concentrating on the dʒ (/j/) phoneme with its four grapheme choices – j, g, dge and ge. There are examples of the pages provided for this phoneme on the CD.

Fantastic Phoneme

Children love this way of remembering spelling choices. The youngest children enjoy listening to the teacher making up silly stories with the keywords for a particular phoneme and are able to do so themselves. This can be used with children as young as five.

The phoneme on each page can be used as a focus, e.g. 'Phoneme of the Week'. The teacher can read the sentence with the class each lesson so that the children have a way of practising, using and remembering different words containing the different graphemes of a particular phoneme.

When using the 'Fantastic Phoneme' with the youngest children, you will be holding very short sessions, probably only focussing the initial sound and grapheme, e.g. the j as in jam, Jack and Jill etc. You would make sure the children are articulating the sound correctly and recognising the shape. Children as young as five may come up with other words such as giant and Gemma and even bridge. It is up to the teacher to decide if these alternative spellings of the sound should be discussed or taught at that point.

As the children progress they should be allowed to 'play' with all the choices and begin to have a 'hook' for the phonemes and their spelling choices. This is where a teacher could utilise the 'Fantastic Phoneme' e.g. 'Giants take ages making jelly jam on bridges'. The children could act out the 'Fantastic Phoneme', saying the words at the same time, so articulating the sound correctly. Slightly older children could take this a stage further by coming up with their own 'Fantastic Phonemes'. One child wrote…'The jolly giant has his jam sarnie on the bridge.'

The children can then draw this story or funny picture, thereby beginning to cement the link between vision and sound that is so important in learning to read, write and spell.

Other work and the above activities allow the children to use all the learning styles, visual, audio and kinaesthetic, to create a 'hook' for the phonemes and some or all of their grapheme choices.

Sometimes with the younger children you may not wish to concentrate on all the graphemes of a phoneme, (e.g. you may only be concentrating on j and g for the dʒ (/j/) phoneme rather than ge and dge as well). The sentences are so short you can just concentrate on the words and graphemes that you want to and could build further lists of relevant words – if the children notice the phoneme appearing in different forms that will be an added bonus and an opening for discussion about their frequency and common position in words. Differentiation is naturally built into the texts and for phonemes with many graphemes we have also provided two sentences. The simplest 'set one' sentences we have provided for phonemes with many graphemes only contain a few simple graphemes.

Alternatively the resource could be used for individual or group study as above. The children could be encouraged to make up words and then sentences of their own using the relevant phoneme.

Grab the Graphemes

This is a simple story for younger children and can also be used as whole class, group, paired or individual work where pupils have to highlight the grapheme choices as they appear when the teacher or one of the children reads out the piece.

Grab the Grapheme can be used in many ways. As commented above, the most basic of uses is to take the text shown below and either as whole class, group, paired or individuals, allow the children find the graphemes for a specific phoneme. 'Wrong phonemes' have been deliberately included in the texts, for example the g in grow in the poem below is the 'correct grapheme' but 'wrong phoneme' in this context, which encourages discussion and debate.

If you put a giant in a cage,

Then you will set him in a rage!

So run away across the bridge,

And hide behind the nearest ridge!

For birds will feed him raspberry jam,

And some jelly-coated ham.

So though it take almost an age,

He will one day out-grow his cage.

And then you'll be sorry…

One extension to this would be for the children to collect and record other words with the same phoneme and grapheme choices. The children could then be encouraged to write and read out similar pieces to gain confidence and experience of using the words in a relevant context. The children could make class books for each phoneme studied.

Because teachers and teaching are most effective when teachers and children are allowed to be creative, this resource can be used in many ways, far more than we could describe here.

Phoneme Fable

This puts key words and then additional words for a particular phoneme and its grapheme choices into a memorable story.

Depending on the age of the children, this story can be shared with the children or they can read it independently.

Activities can include, for example, 'finding the graphemes' and writing a similar story and poem.

The Phoneme Fable can be used in the same way as the Grab the Grapheme texts, whereby as whole class, group, paired or individuals, you allow the children to find the graphemes for a specific phoneme. Depending on age and ability an extension activity may be to put thumbs up when they hear a specific phoneme/grapheme. Groups can 'have' a particular grapheme to make into a differentiated game, e.g. lower attainers 'j' and 'g' and higher attainers 'ge' and 'dge'.

As an advanced exercise the children can be asked to write a piece using the same genre form for a different phoneme, having first made their own list of words. Independently of work on phonemes the different genre forms can also be used for practise in reading and writing.

The 'Phoneme Fable' for the /th/ (ð) (the) phoneme can also be used to learn and practise the difference between the three types of "there" and the additional piece for the two /th/ phonemes can be used to learn to distinguish between the different "ough" words.

All the material can be used as a word level resource, literacy stimulus or brain break for children from reception to year 6, for example drama activities.

The youngest and oldest children love the idea of the Fantastic Phoneme and acting out particular words or a story while also seeing the graphemes, for example, for the b in bird and bb in rabbit some children 'fly' around while others are rabbits eating 'grass'.

Year 6 children have to learn how to spell polysyllabic words with an unstressed vowel in them. Again, they enjoy making up stories and actions for words that will help them to remember the spelling choices. For example: teacher, collar, doctor, measure, zebra, garden, fossil, lion, circus.

The vast majority of the Word recognition and Word structure Objectives from the Primary Framework for Literacy 2006 can be taught and, more importantly, learnt from this resource. For example;

5 year olds

Word recognition Objective

"Read and write one grapheme for the 44 phonemes."

Activity

Read and write j in jam, Jack and Jill

6 year olds

Word recognition Objective

"Recognise and use alternative ways of pronouncing the graphemes already taught, e.g. that the grapheme g is pronounced differently in 'get' and 'gem'."

Activity

Grab the Grapheme focussing on the g in grow compared with g in other words.

7 year olds

Word recognition and Word structure Objective

"Read and spell less common alternative graphemes including trigraphs."

Activity

Differentiated use of Fantastic Phoneme and Grab a Grapheme focussing on the dge trigraphs. Use word list to support children's own list discussing position etc.

8 year olds

Word structure Objective

"Spell unfamiliar words using known conventions including grapheme–phoneme correspondences."

Activity

Use Fantastic Phoneme, Grab a Grapheme and Phoneme Fable to familiarise children with grapheme choices of a particular phoneme to help them develop their spelling of unfamiliar words such as barge, fridge, wedge etc.

9 year olds

Word structure Objective

"Know and apply common spelling rules."

Activity

As above so the children know that the grapheme choices for the phoneme /j/ dʒ are 'j', 'g', 'ge' and 'dge' that 'j' is the most common and 'j' and 'g' are usually at the start of words 'ge' and 'dge' are usually at the end.

10 year olds

Word structure Objective

"Spell words containing unstressed vowels."

Activity

Use the er, ar, or, ure, a, e, i, o, u (I.P.A Symbol: ə L. & S. Symbol: /er/) (short vowel) stories as above.

11 year olds

Word structure Objective

"Use a range of appropriate strategies to edit, proofread and correct spellings in their own work, on paper and on screen."

Activity

Dictate a Fantastic Phoneme, Grab a Grapheme or Phoneme Fable depending on ability. As whole class, groups, pairs or individually check through work focussing on the grapheme choice for the particular phoneme. This can be done on paper or put onto whiteboards.

As you can see, the possibilities for using this resource to cover the objectives are endless and completely in your control. The texts save you hours and hours of writing your own pieces and we have also created a word list that saves you hours of work.

Sample pages for "Fantastic Phonemes"

I.P.A Symbol: dʒ.
L. & S. Symbol: /j/
Common Graphemes Set 1. j, g

Giants enjoy gentle jokes.

Sample pages for "Fantastic Phonemes"

I.P.A. Symbol: ʤ.
L. & S. Symbol: /j/
Common Graphemes Set 2. j, g, ge, dge.

Giants take ages making jelly jam on bridges.

Sample pages for "Grab the Graphemes"

Two short poems about giants

~~~

Giants who live under bridges,
Are subject to attacks from midges.
So they must use a special jelly,
(As advertised on Giant Telly).

To make this gel takes such
an age,
It costs a giant half her wage.
So giants don't live under bridges
And neither do the hungry midges.

~~~

If you put a giant in a cage,
Then you will set him in a rage!

So run away across a bridge,
And hide behind the nearest
fridge!

For birds will feed him raspberry
jam,
And some jelly-coated ham.

So though it take almost an age,
He will one day out-grow his cage.

And then you'll be sorry...

Sample pages for "Phoneme Fables"

There was once a giant called George. Now giants are pretty strange beings, it comes with breathing all that thin air, but George was a giant stranger than most. You see George liked eating bridges. He would get hungry at night-time and go out for a snack and the following day a bridge would be missing, causing massive traffic jams in the local area.

Of course after a while the police realised where the bridges were likely to have gone and decided they would go and call on George and look in his fridge. Sure enough, there in his fridge in a jar was what was left of the bridge set in jelly. (George the giant particularly loved juicy bridge jelly.)

"Look we just can't have this!" shouted Julie the Police Inspector in a rage, waving her police badge at George the Giant. "If you don't stop stealing bridges to put into jars and make into juicy jelly, we're going to have to take you away and put you in cage!"

Well of course George the Giant didn't want to be put in a cage because of a bridge, so he agreed to stop putting them in jars and making them into juicy jelly. He promised to give up half his wage to pay for new bridges, so there wouldn't be traffic jams all over the place any more. As you can imagine Julie was jubilant about this.

Word List

As we had to find and think of words for each phoneme and its graphemes, which sometimes turned out to be quite a chore, we thought it would be useful to include this in the appendix as a resource for you, knowing it would have been useful to us! You could use this resource, for example, to provide a bank of words for the children to write their own versions of the "Fantastic Phonemes", "Grab the Graphemes" or "Phonics Fables". We've tended to make the lists longer where we found it more difficult to think of or find words.

Consonants

International Phonetic Alphabet (I.P.A.) Symbol: b

Letters and Sounds (L. & S.) Symbol: /b/

Common Graphemes b, bb

bull, big, bounce, bird, boat, bun, Bill, bag, Bible, Buddhist, bush, bang, bored, brilliant, dab, scab, grab, sob, habit, bush, bump, balanced, branch

wobble, hobble, bobble, rabbit, bobbed, bobbin, cobble, dabble, dibble, rubble, tabby, jabbed, cobbles, pebble, dabbed, dubbed

- -

I.P.A. Symbol: k

L. & S. Symbol: /k/

Common Graphemes c, k, ck, ch, q

crab, cat, club, camp, can, comb, crib, clap, crept, crust, act, scarf, bacteria, could, concern, corridor, cuddle, craft, class

king, kill, kitten, keep, kit, Koran, kosher, Sikh, kart, kept, kaput, kebab, karat, kayak, knack, kick, ski, skirt, fake, cheek, keep, break, Kevin, Karen, took, take muck, duck, luck, tuck, buck, truck, amuck, suck, sock, hock, mock, sack, back, check, quack, quick, clucking, cuckoo, Patrick, hack, Jack, lack

school, brachiosaurus, echo, ache, Achilles, charisma, character, chaos, chameleon, chimera, chlorine, chord, chorus, Christ, Christchurch, christen

queen, quiet, quiz, quick, quill, quack, mosque, quadrilateral, quail, quake, qualify, quality, quarter, quartz, quay, Quebec, quest, queue, quid, quilt, quit, quote, liquid

- -

I.P.A. Symbol: tʃ

L. & S. Symbol: /ch/

Common Graphemes ch, tch

chair, cheese, teacher, sandwich, cherry, which, search, each, chess, chill, Chinese, chicken, chips, chive, church, chuffed, chair, chain, cheetah, chimney, chase, cheat, children, lunch, hunch, ranch, challenge, punch, munch, choke, chop, Charlie, cheer, check, peaches, leech, such, patch, much, attach

watch, scratch, stretch, hatch, fetch, sketch, witch, wretch, catch, hutch, etch, itch, batch, hatch, patch, pitch, latch, thatch, match, retch, ratchet, eldritch, bitch

- -

I.P.A. Symbol: d

L. & S. Symbol: /d/

Common Graphemes d, dd

dog, dune, din, dart, dam, dear, down, drop, Dad, Hindu, ditch, rid, dove, Dave, Deepti, dustbin, dish, don't, glad, God, quid, held, pad, tad, cad, wad, bad, sad, had, Sid, slid, tidy, day, dinner, do, done, deer, Davina, dimple, duck, wider, end, friend ladder, adder, madder, sadder, Buddhist, gladder, wadded, gadded, nodded, Eddie, Freddie, kiddie, middle, fiddle, piddle, coddle, toddle, bidder, biddable

- -

I.P.A. Symbol: f

L. & S. Symbol: /f/

Common Graphemes f, ff, ph

frog, fry, fish, fridge, freezer, finger, food, fudge, food, film, fin, four, fluff, field, fool, front, France, Friday, roof, fun, feeling, float, friends, Fatima, Farhana

coffee, toffee, fluff, stuff, muff, muffin, staff, scruff, off, affix, daffodil, daffy, boffin, coffin, gaffing, griffin, huffing, buffoon, puffin

phone, dolphin, Phil, Philippa, phoneme, photograph, graph, grapheme, phenomenal, phantom, phoney, philistine, alpha, gopher, orphan, phut

- -

I.P.A. Symbol: g

L. & S. Symbol: /g/

Common Graphemes g, gg

gate, give, peg, leg, girl, goal, great, grim, ghost, Google, sag, bag, tag, wag, game, goat, grill, gap, got, God, gall, gear, beg, goggle, eagle, gaggle, bagel, synagogue, get ghoul, guard

egg, begging, bagging, legging, pegging, sagging, flagging, tagging, tugging, wagging, haggle, waggle ,daggle, mugger, aggressive, aggrieved, beggar, digger, dagger, stagger

NB Also "x" as in exam, examine, example

- -

I.P.A. Symbol: h

L. & S. Symbol: /h/

Common Graphemes h

hand, Harry, Haroon, half, he he, ha ha, huge, hit, how, Hindu, halal, here, hear, head, help, hip, hoe, hobble, hungry, hippo, hate, have, hedgehog, why, hotel, hardly, Henry, horse, her, husband, Helen, horrid, horrify, hound, hose, hot, horn, horizon, hoop, hood, hold, hip, hem, hawk

--- --- --- --- --- --- --- --- --- --- --- --- --- --- --- --- --- --- --- ---

I.P.A. Symbol: dʒ

L. & S. Symbol: /j/

Common Graphemes j, g, ge, dge

jam, job, jog, just, jug, jet, jump, jazz, junk, subject, jar, jelly, juicy, Julie, jubilant, jab, Jack, jacket, jay, jerk, joy, judge, join, Jeep, jaw, Janet, Jamaica, jade, adjective

giant, George, gent, gentle, gee-gee, gel, gem, Gemma, gen, germ, Germany, gin, genius, Genoa, gigantic, ginger, gypsy, gyroscope, ginseng, genuine

age, rage, cage, wage, strange, page, barge, baggage, fudge, cadge, large, gauge, huge, hugely, image, cagey, mage, sage, stage, usage, verge

judge, dodge, badger, hedge, budge, midge, bridge, ridge, fridge, badge, fidget, widget, budge, grudge, drudge, lodge, lodger, edge, gadget, cadge, dodge, wedge, wedged, fudge, grudge, hedge, judge, nudge, kedgeree, ledge

--- --- --- --- --- --- --- --- --- --- --- --- --- --- --- --- --- --- ---

Every Phoneme Covered

I.P.A. Symbol: l

L. & S. Symbol: /l/

Common Graphemes l, ll

lamb, leg, load, left, luggage, lost, loose, lever, Larry, log, lost, lump, lounge, live, alive, level, deal, meal, feel, lumber, loud, lush, little, large, lake, lamp, loo, love, nil, real, realise

all, call, ball, small, tall, bell, hell, well, fell, hall, kill, Bill, Jill, Milly, windowsill, silly, fall, gall, fill, ill, pill, hill, will, dally, alley, really

- -

I.P.A. Symbol: m

L. & S. Symbol: /m/

Common Graphemes m, mm, mb

mouse, man, mum, mumble, Muhammad, manner, mighty, ramble, gamble, Amanda, Mike, Michelle, mosque, pram, tram, tumble, fumble, stumble, yam, shame, dram, am, Sam, ham, wham, sham

hammer, stammer, jamming, hamming, damming, ramming, lamming, ammunition, gamma, mamma, comma, drummer, summit, plummet, commit, lummox

lamb, tomb, comb, sombre, womb, bomb, gumbo, gumboot, gumboil, hombre, rhombus, jamb, combo, kombi, limb, mambo, mamba, numb, number, coomb, combine, combustion, rumba, sombre, zombie

- -

I.P.A. Symbol: n

L. & S. Symbol: /n/

Common Graphemes n, nn, kn

net, now, night, nose, nail, no, not, nave, navy, nice, night, nod, never, net, neck, near, navel, nature, native, Nan, nun, nana, nanny, many

dinner, sinner, winner, thinner, bonny, bunny, canny, banner, conned, gunner, gannet, manner, cannon, cannot, cannibal, pannier, planner, spanner, tanner, canner, runner, inner, sunned, stunned, shunned

knee, kneel, knowledge, knave, knot, knight, knead, knickers, knife, knew, knit, knock, know, knuckle, knucklehead, knoll, knelt, knapsack, knap, knack

- -

I.P.A. Symbol: ŋ

L. & S. Symbol: /ng/

Common Graphemes n, ng

sink, ink, think, wink, blink, clink, link, plink, tinkle, crinkle, winkle, wrinkle, bangle, bank, clank, sank, tank, spank, thank, dank, frank, stank, Inca, tincture

king, ring, sing, fling, doing, mooing, cooing, soaking, floating, bang, wing, long, spring, sting, bring, clang, ding, slung, lung, strong, belong, fang, gang, anger, angle, Angola, Anglo-, angling, strangling, hanging, finger, sling, bangle

- -

I.P.A. Symbol: p

L. & S. Symbol: /p/

Common Graphemes p, pp

peach, purple, panda, important, point, blip, plum, temple, pink, purse, Peter, Petra, Parminder, Parveen, Peru, person, Preston, push, peel, pocket, copy, Japan, pedal, plan, report, Lapland, chapatti, Chippenham

Philippa, hippo, hippy, happy, snappy, sloppy, peppered, zippy, nippy, clipper, nipper, apply, application, apple, applause, appeal, apparel, appetite, approach, dappled, dipper, zipper

---

I.P.A. Symbol: r

L. & S. Symbol: /r/

Common Graphemes r, rr, wr

Rob, race, rail, rain, rung, read, rake, rabbi, racket, radar, radio, rage, radius, railway, rain, raise, raisin, range, rap, rage, rash, error, terror

cherry, merry, berry, ferry, Terry, interrupt, Harry, array, carry, marry, Barry, tarry, err, errand, erratic, error, terror, ferret, burr, curry, worry, parry, carroty, marrow, tomorrow, sorrow

wrap, wrong, wrist, write, wren, writ, written, wrote, wrung, wraith, wrangle, wrapper, wreath, wreck, wrench, wrestle, wriggle, writhe, wry

---

I.P.A. Symbol: s

L. & S. Symbol: /s/

Common Graphemes s, ss, se, c, ce

sun, sea, swim, sleeve, school, discover, synagogue, Sikh, sunken, wrist, sneeze, snail, square, squash, squat, squid, circus, swan, snow, screw, saw, sort, so, success, whilst, sundress, search, son, sauce, bus, distance, instance, symbol, senseless, yes, sausage, assist

profess, fossil, success, sundress, chess, senseless, mess, less, dress, ass, Assam, assault, assess, assist, assort, assassin, assume, bass, bassoon, dissent, frisson, tassel, hassle, gassed, massed, passed, happiness

house, mouse, horse, course, louse, course, copse, douse, dose, close (near), goose, gorse, Morse, morsel, Norse, hearse, rehearse, curse, purse, verse, averse, worse, nurse, cease

civil, circus, success, city, civilisation, cymbal, Cyril, Caesar, Cecil, Cecilia, cicada, cider, El Cid, cinch, cinder, Cinderella, cinema, circle, citation, citrus, cycle, cycling, cyclone, Cyclops, cylinder, cynic, cypress, Cyprus

recent, sauce, ice, distance, instance, mice, trice, nice, twice, cockatrice, rice, lice, price, thrice, sauce, source, cease, Cecil, Cecilia, cell, cement, cent, ceramic, recent, plaice, place

NB Also the -s suffix at the end of words (!) to make them plural also 's as in "teacher's" etc unless the word ends in a vowel or "voiced" consonant (then it's z as in "he's")

NB2 Also the suffix -est as in widest, happiest.

NB3 Also includes x as in relax.

I.P.A. Symbol: ʒ

L. & S. Symbol: /zh/

Common Graphemes s, as in measure

measure, decision, precision, provision, treasure, revision, leisure, collision, vision, pleasure, division, evasion, invasion, azure, closure

— —

I.P.A. Symbol: ʃ

L. & S. Symbol: /sh/

Common Graphemes sh, ti, ch

shark, she'll, ship, shirt, Welsh, English (etc), show, shower, shell, shoe, shower, sheep, kosher, shine, sheet, Shane, shave, shut, sharp, shoot, fish, dish, ship, shed, smash, shin, flush, shift, dash, blush

station, patient, civilisation, national, attention, edition, attraction, translation, transition, election, elation, ambition, compilation, addition, subtraction, multiplication, fraction, relation, invitation, pollution, direction

chef, Charlotte, choux (pastry), chute, parachute, champagne, chivalry, niche, Porsche, machine, sachet, cache, cachet, cloche, Bosch (painter), Richelieu (French statesman)

NB ci, si and ss can sometimes be this phoneme e.g. mission, permission, transmission, profession, efficient, aversion, musician.

— —

I.P.A. Symbol: t

L. & S. Symbol: /t/

Common Graphemes t, tt

tap, tree, two, toe, Tom, Trevor, Tasaf, Torah, temple, tremendous, true, trick, trust, vet, top, tug, but, boat, bat, hat, fat, hit, hot, tapir, tape, tarsier, fit

letter, better, wetter, bitter, go getter, red setter, quitter, fitter, matter, otter, butter, mutter, stutter, shutter, cutter, hitter, hatter, jittery, kitten, mitten, bittern, batter, clatter, clutter

— —

I.P.A. Symbol: ɵ

L. & S. Symbol: /th/

Common Graphemes th, as in thirsty

author, thumb, Earth, thought, throughout, through, thriving, Thirsk, worthless, worth, thick, heath, wreath, birth, think, throat, thing, thin, throw, threw, south, north, eighth, ninth, thirteenth, eleventh, third, thirst, three, thrash, thread, throne, throng, thief, thrush, thrust, theme, thank, strength, path

— —

I.P.A. Symbol: ð

L. & S. Symbol: /th/

Common Graphemes th, as in the

though, they, whether, weather, other, there, their, they're, them, feather, this, the, thimble, heather, that, clothes, gather, those, than, then, themselves, thereby, therefore, thy, bother, brother, wither, father, fathom, these, bathe, lather

— —

I.P.A. Symbol: v

L. & S. Symbol: /v/

Common Graphemes v, ve

voice, vile, violent, victory, vase, view, van, vent, vacant, vole, vote, visit, oven, over, survive, van, vet, vest, vicar, vex, vivid, visit, velvet, vague, vain, Valencia, valve, variety, vast, vault, veil, vein, device, evening

NB Some words have "ve", particularly at the beginning of words but the "e" is part of another phoneme.

believe, sleeve, conceive, perceived, alive, survive, arrive, dwarves, valve, deceive, received, Steve, live, hive, strive, chive, Clive, clove, rove, drove, strove, stove, hove, love, dove

— —

I.P.A. Symbol: w

L. & S. Symbol: /w/ (or /wh/ for regional pronounciation of 'wh')

Common Graphemes w, wh, u

(Note – The u is the one that always comes after q.)

water, won, week, win, will, wet, weather, wish, well, wishing, wash, William, wind, ware, weak, wind, wigwam, wag, web, swim, well, wept, went, west, wig, swell, swam, wet

wheel, why, what, when, where, whether, whip, whipping, white, whisper, which, wham, whoosh, wheel, wheat, while, white, why,whisker, whimper, whisk, whale, wham, whirl, whiz

quilt, quickly, queen, quiz, quill, quirk, quit, quick, liquid, quack, quest, quite, quiet, quarter, quadrilateral, qualification, qualify, quash, queasy, quilt, quench, quip, quaint, quoits, quote

— —

I.P.A. Symbol: j

L. & S. Symbol: /y/

Common graphemes y

(Note – as in yes and yacht but not as in why or choppy.)

yet, year, yearn, yawn, yell, yowl, yap, yapping, yelp, yak, yank, yacht, yam, yard, yes, yesterday, year, yew, yellow, yeah, yeast, yeti, yap, yarn, yield, young, youth, you, York, yum-yum, Yasser, yeoman

——————————————————————————————————————

I.P.A. Symbol: z

L. & S. Symbol: /z/

Common Graphemes z, zz, ze, s, se

zoo, zebra, zippy, zip, razor, gaze, blazer, whiz, zip, zigzag, zap, zany, zeal, zero, Zeus, zinc, zing, hazy, crazy, lazy, zone, zoom, Zulu, Zimbabwe, zodiac, Zaire, Zambia, brazier, Brazil, kazoo, hazelnut

fuzzy, fizz, buzz, fuzz, tizzy, pizzazz (or pizzazz or pzazz), Brazzaville (capital of Republic of Congo), jazzed, jazz, jazzes, razzle-dazzle, razzmatazz (or razzamatazz)

NB The two z's in pizza are t then s phoneme.

sneeze, freeze, wheeze, breeze, daze, craze, haze, maze, doze, adze, blaze, baize, braze, faze, gaze, graze, laze, lazed, oozed, raze, size, amaze

reason, visa, his, civilisation, laser, "Phaser", museum, visible, vis-à-vis, goes, clothes, does, ways, cubism, do-se-do, doesn't, fuselage, has, has-been, hawse, Los Angeles, music

NB Also the -s suffix at the end of words to make them plural. Also 's as in "he's" etc if the word ends in a vowel or "voiced" consonant (otherwise it's s as in "teacher's").

because, use, please, cheese, Louise, disease, phase, pose, hose, abuse, amuse, use, arouse, cause, close (shut), ease, rouse, fuse, nose, guise, hawser, vase, lose, muse, nose, pause, rise, rose, ruse, raise

-- -- -- -- -- -- -- -- -- -- -- -- -- -- -- -- -- -- -- --

Vowels and Diphthongs

I.P.A. Symbol: æ

L. & S. Symbol: /a/

Common Graphemes a as in ant

(short vowel)

fat, man, mad, jam, bat, mat, rat, bag, cabbage, calendar, can, ant, rabbit, ambush, Andes, Allah, cat, ladder, scratch, hand, jam, hammer, lamb, Carla, panda, tap, aboriginal, Anglo-Australian, Antarctic, anaconda, anticipate, act, arch, ambrosia, ancestral, ancestor, amazing, antenna, aluminium, Angola, Afghanistan, altitude, attitude, alto, Africa, Aloe Vera, and, dramatic, animals, amnesty, attack, accidents, annoying, assistant, anxiety, archaeology, pant, elephant, scant, rant, blackcurrant, pendant, repentant, arrogant, expectant, assistant, celebrant, deodorant, anti-aircraft, anaesthetic, anticipate, anticlimax, Alison, Andy, Adam, Amina

-- -- -- -- -- -- -- -- -- -- -- -- -- -- -- -- -- -- -- --

I.P.A. Symbol: eɪ

L. & S. Symbol: /ae/

Common Graphemes a, a-e, ai, ay

"long a" (diphthong)

baby, bacon, basic, bass (note), dado, danger, dangerous, Davy lamp, Gaelic, gauge, papal, paste, pasteboard, patience, patient

gate, name, wake, mate, take, hate, tape, made, cake, tale, wave, date, late, cave, game, gave, flame, rake, came, lake, same, ate, save, grape, safe, snake, bake, baker, Bakewell tart, base, baseball, basement, dale, dame, Dane, gale, gape, gaze

rain, trail, main, sail, saint, snail, gain, wait, jail, paid, hail, rail, brain, grain, drain, vain, tail, pain, laid, waist, painter, strain, afraid, Spain, train, nail, chain, mail, daisy, bail, bailiff, bait, gain, pail, paint

may, pay, Hurray, pray, tray, staying, stray, yesterday, Monday, Tuesday, lay, say, stay, clay, away, crayon, play, today, foray, hay, stay, spray, maybe, bay, bayonet, Bayeux Tapestry

NB Also "-eigh" as in weight, sleigh, eight, freight.

I.P.A. Symbol: eə

L. & S. Symbol: /air/

Common Graphemes air, are

(diphthong)

fairy, hair, pair, air, Claire, lair, fair, stair, flair, chair, cairn, dairy, airy, hairy, stair, repair, despair, aircraft share, caretaker, rare, square, hare, care, dare, area, scare, fare, glare, mare, ware, stare, bare, aware, beware, mare, snare, pare

NB Also "ea" as in bear, wear

- -

I.P.A. Symbol: a

L. & S. Symbol: /ar/

Common Graphemes a, ar

(long vowel)

banana, staff, calm, nana, after, asked, halal, can't, father, lava, last, pass, password, passport, drama, heart, panama, bathroom, llama, castle, guava, sultana, pyjamas, alms, aircraft

hard, start, spark, harm, car, cart, bar, ajar, jar, farm, started, tar, mark, mar, argue, artist, parting, arm, lard, radar, lark, catarrh, large, Arthur, garden, march, parking, shark, sharp, larva, start, dark, park, smart, tar, star, far, scarves, Arsenal, Arnold, Arthur, heart, archaeology, arch

- -

I.P.A. Symbol: e

L. & S. Symbol: /e/

Common Graphemes e, ea

(short vowel)

men, bed, ten, net, wet, Ned, jet, pet, hen, Ben, wedding, fed, led, Mediterranean, red, teddy, Ted, beck, beckon, bedbug, bedding, bedlam, Bedouin, beg, belch, belfry, Belgium, debit, debris, Mecca, pebble, Helen, helicopter, cell

weather, sweat, bread, dead, head, lead (metal), deadline, deaf, deafen, death, feather, heather, heavy, leather, meadow, measure, peasant, ready, health

- -

I.P.A. Symbol: i

L. & S. Symbol: /ee/

Common Graphemes e, ea, ee, ey, y

"long e" (long vowel)

me, be, he, Hebrew, helium, helix, bebop, being, beta, alphabet, cedar, debug, decaf, decent, decode, decompress, defrost, pecan, peony, people, sequence, sequin, evil

read, east, mean, clean, clear, heat, near, beans, beach, beak, cream, leak, eat, meat, each, heat, reach, team, read, heap, peas, peach, leap, tea, peanut, stream, seat, cheap, sea, lead (guide), bead, cease, peat

queen, sheep, tree, meet, asleep, greed, need, heel, street, bleed, see, green, indeed, feed, week, deep, jeep, speed, greedy, feet, beef, seem, bee, beech, beef, beep, beetle, Ceefax, decree, deed, degree, peep

hockey, key, valley, monkey, honey, jockey, donkey, phoney, money, baloney, blarney, Orkney, gooney, gurneys, journey, jersey, Rooney, storey

pony, agony, any, bony, corny, felony, irony, loony, lemony, peony, stormy, serenely

NB Also "i" with "e" as in magazine, receive, siege.

I.P.A. Symbol: ɪə

L. & S. Symbol: /ear/

Common Graphemes ear, eer

(diphthong)

year, appeared, spear, ear, near, dear, fear, gear, hear, tear, clear, rear, smear, sear, Lear (writer of limericks/Shakespearian character) Shakespeare, disappear

deer, beer, cheer, peer, steer, veer, leer, jeer, seer, seer, freer, sneer, steer, steerage, meerkat

--- --- --- --- --- --- --- --- --- --- --- --- --- --- --- --- --- --- --- ---

I.P.A. Symbol: ə

L. & S. Symbol: /er/

Common Graphemes er, ar, or, ure, a, e, i, o, u

(short vowel)

Quaker, quaver, gallery, kipper, killer, hammer, bigger, baker, farmer, pepper, father, mother, sister, teacher, ladder, hammer, caterpillar, power, letter, feather, water, laser, tiger, water, waiter, warder, after, further, worker, silver, wander, water, colander, potter, cleaner, reaper, knocker, bitter

hear, collar, rear, dollar, caterpillar, clear, fear, disappear, pillar, polar, pollard, leeward

doctor, actor, factor, factory, factorise, tractor, pastor, pastoral

measure, treasure, leisure, pleasure, gesture, posture, moisture, closure, feature, nature

zebra, vanilla, giant, panda, banana, larva, lava, attune, amazing, astounding, astonishing, drama, dramatic, agog, avenge, available, address, aerial, Panama, affair, pupa, nana, disappear, baboon, Kenya, pillar, vacate, vacation, Inca, vagabond, warrant, colossal, alone, alpha, poppadom, lima, llama

garden, kitten, killer, knocker, mitten, bitten, bittern, bitter, sicken, silken, warren, the, dolmen, caterer, pollen

fossil, fossils

lion, station, to, station, patient, civilisation, national, attention, edition, attraction, translation, transition, election, elation, ambition, attraction, compilation, addition, subtraction, multiplication, fraction, relation, invitation, pollution, direction, bacon, vocabulary, collect, nation, dollop, carrot, London

circus, upon, colossus, colour, opossum, arbour, mollusc, Saturday, Saturn, Muhammad, Claudius (Roman emperor), Nureyev (Russian dancer), Sibelius (composer)

NB. Also the "u" in words with the suffix "–ous" e.g. miraculous, ominous, envious, glorious.

- -

I.P.A. Symbol: ɜ

L. & S. Symbol: /ur/

Common Graphemes er, ir, or, ur

(long vowel)

fern, herb, perch, stern, her, herd, serve, perm, perch, herbal, percolate, perfect, perfume, perforate, perky, sterling, Serb, sermon, serpent, Herculean, hermit, stern

circle, thirty, shirt, sir, smirk, birthday, dirt, twirl, firm, swirl, thirteen, flirting, bird, girl, stir, chirp, thirst, first, birth, third, fir, skirt, twirl, stirring, shirk, firmly, flirt work, worm, working, worker, world, worse, worship, word, worry, worth, worn, Wordsworth

turn, burn, surf, fur, turf, hurt, burnt, burst, church, churn, Saturn, curl, nurse, purse, curve, murder, hurting, hamburger, beefburger, Thursday, Saturday, purr, turnip, purple, burglar, curly, turned, hurtful, further, turkey

NB Also "–ear" e.g. learn, search, earth, heard, earl, earn.

- --

I.P.A. Symbol: ɪ

L. & S. Symbol: /i/

Common Graphemes i, e

(short vowel)

sit, tin, pin, sin, bin, din, gin, kin, in, bulletin, zip, it, bit, lip, wig, is, pig, Tim, important, inch, ignore, ill, imam, imagine, indeed, ink, sink, inside, intend, Islam, chin, cinema, fin, him, hint, hip, history, ticket, wicket, cricket, tie

socket, pocket, rocket, locket, docket, comet, poet, bullet, baronet, bucket, jacket, machete, packet, racket, ticket, wicket, cricket, wanted

- --

I.P.A. Symbol: aɪ

L. & S. Symbol: /ie/

Common Graphemes i, i-e, igh, y

"long i" (diphthong)

tiger, tidy, Siamese, siding, sidle, idle, Bible, sign, Simon, tie, tidal, Titan, Titanic, tithe, title, pie, piebald, pint, piping, pirate, dive, Tai

wire, time, five, fire, live, life, wide, pile, ripe, hive, drive, nine, white, wipe, shine, tide, side, prize, mine, quite, line, wife, smile, kite, like, bike, time, hide, admire, hire, spire, size, tile, tire, pike, pile, aisle

sigh, night, light, lightning, thigh, sight, tight, right, fright, slight, high, bright, flight, might, slight, plight, alight, fight, knight

dry, fly, spy, my, by, dry, shy, sky, why, flying, frying, drying, myself, crying, try, July, satisfying, python, pylon, type, nylon, buying, guy, rye

— —

I.P.A. Symbol: ɒ

L. & S. Symbol: /o/

Common Graphemes o, a

(short vowel)

box, on, fox, Tom, got, lot, not, fog, frog, dog, coffee, dolphin, fossil, rocket, bonny, agog, bog, cog, hop, hot, odd, gone, on, pop, poppy, grog, hedgehog, jog, clog, log

swan, watch, was, want, wasp, what, wan, wand, wander, wanting, warren, wad, waffle, waft, wallet, wallop, wallow, wally, Warren, warrant, wash, Watson

— —

I.P.A. Symbol: əʊ

L. & S. Symbol: /oe/

Common Graphemes o, oa, o-e, ow

"long o" (diphthong)

nose, no, go, so, ocean, oh, old, cold, hello, Colchester, toe, foe, vocal, jojoba, cola, logo, local, poet, poem, pogo, podium, Poland, polar, poky, Poirot (fictional detective), Puerto Rico, gold, gross

croak, Joan, moat, soap, bloated, boat, coast, coal, loaf, toad, croak, moan, load, roam, cloak, throat, boats, soak, coach, road, foam, roast, groan, goat, cockroach, poach, goal, toast, coat, stoat, oak, gloat, soap, oats, foal, float, afloat, oath

bone, joke, note, those, hose, smoke, lonely, vote, doze, coke, stroke, rode, cope, hope, woke, lone, stone, cone, poke, choke, rope, pole, close, nose, globe, spoke, home, mole, broke, rose, slope, alone, drove, grope

low, snow, glow, follow, blow, rowing, arrow, window, blowing, crow, elbow, own, borrow, bowl, throw, slowest, tomorrow, owner, yellow, marrow, grow, shadow, lowest, throw, slow, mow, show, pillow, flow, row

- -

I.P.A. Symbol: ɔɪ

L. & S. Symbol: /oi/

Common Graphemes oi, oy

(diphthong)

poison, avoid, choice, coin, oil, foil, spoil, soil, toil, oink, oily, noise, coil, boil, noisy, ointment, boil, toilet, point, joined, voice, point, joint, joist, hoist, moist, poise, voile, quoits, void

loyal, toy, Roy, joy, boy, Ahoy, annoy, Savoy, employ, enjoying, royal, destroy, soy, coy, buoy, buoyant, cloy, ploy, Troy, voyage

— — — — — — — — — — — — — — — — — — — —

I.P.A. Symbol: ʊ

L. & S. Symbol: /oo/

Common Graphemes u, oo

(short vowel)

stood, book, foot, wood, good, took, shook, hood, brook, hook, cook, look, cookie, cooking, wool, woof, nook, rook, crook, brook, goody–goody

bull, Buddha, Buddhism, full, fulfil, Muslim, pussy-cat, push, pushy, put, pull, pudding, hummus

NB Also the "u" in the suffix "–ful" as in beautiful, forgetful, useful.

— — — — — — — — — — — — — — — — — — — —

I.P.A. Symbol: u

L. & S. Symbol: /ue/

Common Graphemes oo, ew, ue

"long u" (long vowel)

spoon, pool, loot, moon, food, root, loop, smooth, spoon, balloon, noon, shoot, hoop, roof, zoo, boot, tooth, moon, soon, hoot, loo, coo, cooed, cool, doom, fool, noodle, noon, noose, bloom, loot, toot, room, scoop, school, too

crew, brew, screw, few, pew, skew, blew, drew, view, grew, flew, chewing, threw, new, news, stew, newspaper, dew, newt

blue, clue, true, glue, Sue, due, cue, argue, value, fuel, fuels, barbecue, continue, rescue

NB "u–e" can be the same phoneme e.g. rude, flute, rule, salute, prune, June, tune, nude, tube, duke, rude, use, huge, cute, as can "ou" as in you.

— —

I.P.A. Symbol: ɔ

L. & S. Symbol: /or/ for 'or', 'oor' & 'ar' /au/ for 'au', 'aw' & 'a'

Common Graphemes or, a, au, aw, oor, ar

(long vowel)

storm, torn, form, born, fork, Torah, sworn, or, porcelain, porch, pork, pore, port, adore, tore, score, store, core, shore, chore, more, stork, York, cork, bore, galore, ordinary, fort, afford, morning, bore, Koran

ball, water, walk, call, war, wall, chalk, talk, tall, small, hall, Balti, Baltic, ballpark, all, always, fall, Falklands, gall, gallstone, hallmark, watermark, pall, waltz, bald haul, Saul, sauce, taught, taunt, jaunting, vault, vaunt, launch, laud, pause, Paul, August, astronaut, launch, cause, laundry, fault, autumn, maul, daub, bauble, cauldron, caution

outlaw, draw, paw, spawn, lawn, saw, law, flaw, drawn, hawk, claw, jaw, sprawl, dawdle, shawl, sawdust, straw, trawler, pawn, raw, prawn, yawn, yaw, bawl, crawl, drawl, dawn, awl, awning

door, moor, floor, poor, poorly, boor, doorstep, doorway, spoor

NB moor, boor, poor and spoor can alternatively use the ʊə /oor/ phoneme.

warn, warp, warm, warder, war, wart, warble, warthog, Warsaw

NB Also "–ou" such as pour, four, court, mourn, journey.

I.P.A. Symbol: aʊ

L. & S. Symbol: /ow/

Common graphemes ou, ow

(diphthong)

shout, loud, count, trout, sound, house, outside, mouse, spout, clout, spouse, hour, cloud, mountain, about, hound, sound, round, found, proud, couch, blouse, ground, our, south

power, crowd, now, cow, owl, how, towel, trowel, town, clown, frown, brown, crown, howl, shower, fowl, drown, allow, scowl, gown, sow, avow, wow, however, down, jowl, crowd

------

I.P.A. Symbol: ʌ

L. & S. Symbol: /u/

Common Graphemes u, o

(short vowel)

bus, duck, sun, thumb, trump, up, adult, pus, musk, must, bust, crust, lust, just, rust, trust, such, suck, sudden, sucker, suss, cuss, fuss, button, butter, public, publish, puddle, puff-adder, pun, cut, gut, hut, jutting, mutt, nut, rut, tut tut, dust, mud, much, sum, fun, pup, bun, mum, pub

love, glove, wonderful, wondrous, come, comfort, monk, mother, monkey, Monday, money, other, brother, someone, something, dove, flood, blood, dozen, done

— —

Index for Word List

Phoneme / Consonants	Page	Phoneme / Consonants	Page
I.P.A. Symbol: b. L. & S. Symbol: /b/ Common Graphemes b, bb	23	I.P.A. Symbol: p. L. & S. Symbol: /p/ Common Graphemes p, pp	29
I.P.A. Symbol: k. L. & S. Symbol: /k/ Common Graphemes c, k, ck, ch, q	23	I.P.A. Symbol: r. L. & S. Symbol: /r/ Common Graphemes r, rr, wr	29
I.P.A. Symbol: tʃ. L. & S. Symbol: /ch/ Common Graphemes ch, tch	24	I.P.A. Symbol: s. L. & S. Symbol: /s/ Common Graphemes s, ss, se, c, ce	30
I.P.A. Symbol: d. L. & S. Symbol: /d/ Common Graphemes d, dd	25	I.P.A. Symbol: ʒ. L. & S. Symbol: /zh/ Common Graphemes s, as in measure	31
I.P.A. Symbol: f. L. & S. Symbol: /f/ Common Graphemes f, ff, ph	25	I.P.A. Symbol: ʃ. L. & S. Symbol: /sh/ Common Graphemes sh, ti, ch	31
I.P.A. Symbol: g. L. & S. Symbol: /g/ Common graphemes g, gg	25	I.P.A. Symbol: t. L. & S. Symbol: /t/ Common Graphemes t, tt	32
I.P.A. Symbol: h. L. & S. Symbol: /h/ Common Graphemes h	26	I.P.A. Symbol: Ɵ. L. & S. Symbol: /th/ Common Graphemes th, as in thirsty	32
I.P.A. Symbol: dʒ. L. & S. Symbol: /j/ Common Graphemes j, g, ge, dge	26	I.P.A. Symbol: ð. L. & S. Symbol: /th/ Common Graphemes th, as in the	32
I.P.A. Symbol: l. L. & S. Symbol: /l/ Common Graphemes l, ll	27	I.P.A. Symbol: v. L. & S. Symbol: /v/ Common Graphemes v, ve	33
I.P.A. Symbol: m. L. & S. Symbol: /m/ Common Graphemes m, mm, mb	27	I.P.A. Symbol: w. L. & S. Symbol: /w/ (or /wh/ for regional pronunciation of 'wh'.) Common Graphemes w, wh, u	33
I.P.A. Symbol: n. L. & S. Symbol: /n/ Common Graphemes n, nn, kn	28	I.P.A. Symbol: j. L. & S. Symbol: /y/ Common Graphemes y	34
I.P.A. Symbol: ŋ. L. & S. Symbol: /ng/ Common Graphemes n, ng	28	I.P.A. Symbol: z. L. & S. Symbol: /z/ Common Graphemes z, zz, ze, s, se	34

Phoneme Vowels and Diphthongs	Page	Phoneme Vowels and Diphthongs	Page
I.P.A. Symbol: æ L. & S. Symbol: /a/ Common Graphemes a as in ant (short vowel)	35	I.P.A. Symbol: aɪ L. & S. Symbol: /ie/ Common Graphemes i, i-e, igh, y "long i" (diphthong)	42
I.P.A Symbol: eɪ L. & S. Symbol: /ae/ Common Graphemes a, a-e, ai, ay "long a" (diphthong)	36	I.P.A. Symbol: ɒ L. & S. Symbol: /o/ Common Graphemes o, a (short vowel)	42
I.P.A. Symbol: eə L. & S. Symbol: /air/ Common Graphemes air, are (diphthong)	36	I.P.A. Symbol: əʊ L. & S. Symbol: /oe/ Common Graphemes o, oa, o-e, ow "long o" (diphthong)	43
I.P.A. Symbol: a: L. & S. Symbol: /ar/ Common Graphemes a, ar (long vowel)	37	I.P.A. Symbol: ɔɪ L. & S. Symbol: /oi/ Common Graphemes oi, oy (diphthong)	44
I.P.A. Symbol: e L. & S. Symbol: /e/ Common Graphemes e, ea (short vowel)	37	I.P.A Symbol: ʊ L. & S. Symbol: /oo/ Common Graphemes u, oo (short vowel)	44
I.P.A. Symbol: i: L. & S. Symbol: /ee/ Common Graphemes e, ea, ee, ey, y "long e" (long vowel)	38	I.P.A. Symbol: u: L. & S. Symbol: /ue/ Common Graphemes oo, ew, ue "long u" (long vowel)	45
I.P.A. Symbol: ɪə L. & S. Symbol: /ear/ Common Graphemes ear, eer (diphthong)	39	I.P.A. Symbol: ɔ: L. & S. Symbol: /or/ for 'or', 'oor' & 'ar' / au/ for 'au', 'aw' & 'a' Common Grapheme or, a, au, aw, oor, ar (long vowel)	45
I.P.A. Symbol: ə L. & S. Symbol: /er/ Common Graphemes er, ar, or, ure, a, ,e, i, o, u (short vowel)	39	I.P.A. Symbol: aʊ L. & S. Symbol: /ow/ Common Graphemes ou, ow (diphthong)	46
I.P.A. Symbol: ɜ: L. & S. Symbol: /ur/ Common Graphemes er, ir, or, ur (long vowel)	40	I.P.A. Symbol: ʌ L. & S. Symbol: /u/ Common Graphemes u, o (short vowel)	47
I.P.A. Symbol: ɪ L. & S. Symbol: /i/ Common Graphemes i, e, (short vowel)	41		

Summary of Phonemes and their Graphemes provided in Every Phoneme Covered

Sets 1 and 2 appear in the **Fantastic Phoneme** sentences. Set 1 provides a simplified range of graphemes and Set 2 provides the full range of the most common graphemes. The full range of common graphemes is utilised in the **Grab the Grapheme** paragraphs and the page long **Phonics Fable** pieces.

Letters and Sounds Symbol	I.P.A. Symbol (used in most dictionaries)	Graphemes used
Consonants		
/b/	b	b, bb
/k/	k	Set 1. c, k, q Set 2. c, k, ck, ch, q
/ch/	tʃ	ch, tch
/d/	d	d, dd
/f/	f	Set 1. f, ff Set 2. f, ff, ph
/g/	g	g, gg
/h/	h	h
/j/	dʒ	Set 1. j, g Set 2. j, g, ge, dge
/l/	l	l, ll
/m/	m	Set 1. m, mm Set 2. m, mm, mb

Letters and Sounds Symbol	I.P.A. Symbol (used in most dictionaries)	Graphemes used
/n/	n	Set 1. n, nn Set 2. n, nn, kn
/ng/	ŋ	n, ng
/p/	p	p, pp
/r/	r	Set 1. r, rr Set 2. r, rr, wr
/s/	s	Set 1. s, ss, c Set 2. s, ss, se, c, ce
/zh/	ʒ	s (as in measure)
/sh/	ʃ	Set 1. sh Set 2. sh, ti, ch
/t/	t	t, tt
/th/	ө	th (as in thirsty)
/th/	ð	th (as in the)
/v/	v	v, ve
/w/ (or /wh/ in regional pronunciation of "wh")	w	Set 1. w Set 2. w, wh, u
/y/	j	y
/z/	z	Set 1. z, ze Set 2. z, zz, ze, s, se

Summary of Phonemes and their Graphemes

Letters and Sounds Symbol	I.P.A. Symbol (used in most dictionaries)	Graphemes used
Vowels and Diphthongs		
/a/ (short vowel)	æ	a (as in ant)
/ae/ ("long a" diphthong)	eɪ	Set 1. a, ay Set 2. a, a–e, ai, ay
/air/ (diphthong)	eə	air, are
/ar/ (long vowel)	a:	a, ar
/e/ (short vowel)	e	e, ea
/ee/ ("long e" long vowel)	i:	Set 1. e, ee Set 2. e, ea, ee, ey, y
/ear/ (diphthong)	ɪə	ear, eer
/er/ (short vowel)	ə	Set 1. er, or Set 2. er, ar, or, ure, a, e, i, o, u
/ur/ (long vowel)	ɜ:	er, ir, or, ur
/i/ (short vowel)	ɪ	i, e
/ie/ ("long i" diphthong)	aɪ	Set 1. i, y Set 2. i, i–e, igh, y

Letters and Sounds Symbol	I.P.A. Symbol (used in most dictionaries)	Graphemes used
/o/ (short vowel)	ɒ	o, a
/oe/ ("long o" diphthong)	əʊ	Set 1. o, ow Set 2. o, oa, o-e, ow
/oi/ (diphthong)	ɔɪ	oi, oy
/oo/ (short vowel)	ʊ	u, oo
/ue/ ("long u" long vowel)	u:	Set 1. ue Set 2. oo, ew, ue
/or/ (for "or", "oor" & "ar") /au/ (for "au", "aw" & "a") (long vowel)	ɔ:	Set 1. or, au Set 2. or, a, au, aw, oor, ar
/ow/ (dipthong)	aʊ	ou, ow
/u/ (short vowel)	ʌ	u, o
/ee/ ("long e" long vowel)	i:	Set 1. ee, ee Set 2. e, ea, ee, ey, y

Teaching Order

The following represents one suggestion regarding the order in which the phonemes are presented. It is based upon the overall sequence of teaching outlined by the Letters and Sounds programme

Group 1
/s/, /m/, /k/, /t/, /g/, /h/

Group 2
/l/, /n/, /d/, /sh/, /ch/

Group 3
/a/, /e/, /i/, /o/, /u/, /f/, /b/, /r/, /j/, /p/, /th/, /ng/

Group 4
/v/, /w/, /y/, /z/

Group 5
/ae/, /ee/, /ie/, /oe/, /ue/, /ar/, /or/, /ur/, /oi/, /oo/, /ow/

Group 6
/er/, /au/, /air/, /ear/

Every Phoneme Covered